Bargello Is Easy

Bargello Is Easy

by Peri Wolfman

Published in association
with *Parade Magazine*

GROSSET & DUNLAP
Publishers   New York

To Aunt Mil, who gave me my first needle

Contents

What Is Bargello?

Traditionally Bargello is the art of Florentine canvas work. Does that answer your question? No.

O.K. Bargello is vertical stitches worked on single-mesh canvas. Sometimes a stitch goes over two threads of canvas, sometimes over six threads, but most commonly over four threads.

Today you can do Bargello in the most modern, bright colors using traditional Florentine patterns, or you can use traditional colors on new and modern patterns. You can use Bargello stitches on a painted needlepoint canvas (flowers, animals, landscapes), or you can use a combination of Bargello stitches to create a patchwork of pattern.

Using your imagination and this basic book, the application of Bargello is unlimited.

1

Color

With Bargello the number of color combinations is limitless. You can use anything and everything. Bargello patterns are traditionally worked in many shades (four to six) of one color, but wonderful things happen when you use your imagination.

Hot colors: Reds • fuchsias • oranges • purples • repeat

Cool colors: Turquoises • royal blues • lavenders • mauves • repeat
Kelly • turquoise • royal • mint • repeat

Naturals: Wheat • camel • taupe • alabaster • repeat

Flags: White • red • white • blue • white • red • repeat
Green • red • yellow • repeat

Shadings: 3 shades each of lots of bright colors (Example: 3 shades each of yellows, oranges, pinks, and purples); 4 or 5 shades of one color plus an accent color (Example: 5 shades of blue and 1 bright red); 4 to 6 shades of one lovely color

Materials

Assemble your materials: canvas, yarn, needles. Use the best quality. You're going to put many hours into your Bargello; you want it to look beautiful and last a lifetime.
  The next pages will tell you:

♥   What type to buy

▲   In what quantities it is sold

♣   How much it costs

Canvas (some people call it scrim)

♥ Mono canvas is the thing to use for Bargello.
Mono means a single thread (as opposed to Pene-
lope or double-thread canvas). The number of the
canvas corresponds to the *holes per inch*.
Number 12 canvas has twelve holes per inch.
Number 14 canvas has fourteen holes per inch.
I think No. 12 is ideal for Bargello.

▲ Most canvas is forty inches wide and is sold by the
yard. However, you can buy parts of a yard in many
shops.

♣ The best grade costs about $8.00 a yard and a yard
goes a long way.

Yarn (use all wool!)

♥ Persian yarn is the finest traditional type. It comes
in sixty-four color groups with five shades of each
color. The variety is mind boggling! Each strand of
Persian yarn is three ply (loosely twisted together).
Use all three ply together for Bargello. If you are
unable to buy Persian yarn, you can use knitting
worsted. However, the colors will be limited.

▲ Persian yarn is usually sold by the ounce with about twenty-four strands (each sixty inches long) per ounce.

♣ It costs about $1.20 per ounce. You can usually buy as little as a quarter of an ounce of a color.

Needle

♥ Use a tapestry needle. It has a blunt point (so it won't split the threads of the canvas) and a large enough eye to thread wool. Losing a needle in the middle of the night and not having a spare is a frustrating experience, so buy a few.

I like a No. 18 tapestry for No. 12 canvas and a No. 20 tapestry for No. 14 canvas.

▲ Tapestry needles are sold singly or in packages of all one size or a variety of sizes.

♣ Loose, they are about five cents each.

Extras

You will also need:

1. A small pair of scissors with a sharp nose for cutting yarn and removing mistakes.
2. A large all-purpose pair of scissors (you probably have an adequate pair around the house) for cutting canvas.
3. Masking tape for the edges of the canvas.
4. An *indelible* laundry marking pen for marking the size of your Bargello area on the canvas.

What Will the Total Cost Be?

Let's start with a small pillow or sampler. You'll need:

Canvas: Buy one-half yard of No. 12 (this can be cut into
    smaller pieces) $4.00

                      or

    Buy an eighteen-inch square of No. 12 (if the shop sells
    it this way) $2.00

Yarn: Buy five ounces of Persian (any colors you love)
                                                    $6.25

Needles: Buy three (be a sport) $ .15

Tape: Buy a roll of masking tape (you'll have it for many
    canvases) $2.50

                      or

    Have the shop tape your canvas (some shops will, some
    won't) $ .50

The most your pillow or sampler will cost is $12.90
with supplies for more projects

The least it will cost is $8.90
if you buy the best materials for one pillow

Preparing Your Canvas

Cut your canvas between two lines, one and a half
inches larger on all sides than you want your finished
piece to be.

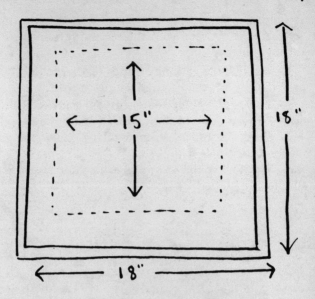

Using an indelible fine-tip marking pen, draw an outline approximately the size you want your finished work.

Place masking tape on edge and fold over. Do this on all sides so canvas won't ravel and your yarn won't catch and fray on the rough edges.

8

Thread your needle by folding the yarn in half and squeezing it between your thumb and forefinger. Press it through the eye.

If your yarn is in long strands (sixty inches), cut it in half. Thirty inches is a good length to work with.

1. To start, find the center of your canvas. Bring your needle up from the back of the canvas to the front.

2. Hold the end of yarn on the back of the canvas. Never knot!

3. Work over the yarn end with your first couple of stitches.

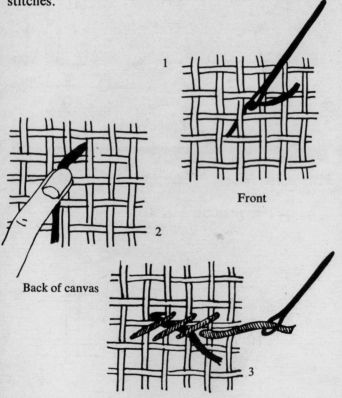

Front

Back of canvas

4. To end the yarn when it is getting short, put your needle through to the back of your canvas and run the needle (and yarn) under several stitches. Then cut it close to the canvas.

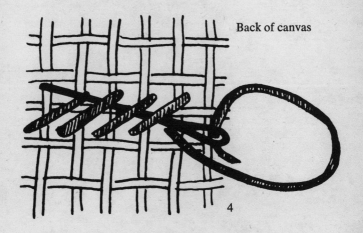

Back of canvas

4

Basic Flame Stitch

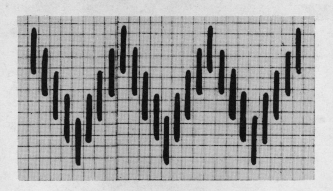

Here is a single line of a basic *flame stitch*. The next pages will show you step by step how to "set up" your first line of Bargello, then how to create your pattern.

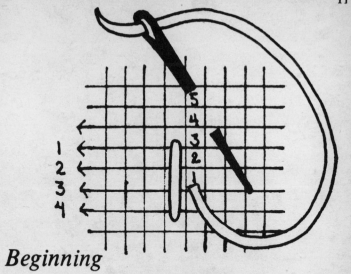

Beginning

The stitch is vertical! It is worked over four threads of canvas. Count five holes including the hole your yarn comes out of and the hole your needle goes into. Start the first row in the center of your canvas.

Moving Up

With each new stitch you move one row to the right (or left) and up three holes (under two threads), bringing

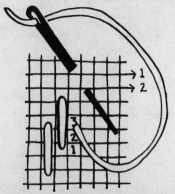

your needle up through the third hole, counting from the last hole of the previous stitch. Each stitch, like your first stitch, covers five holes of canvas. This is always the way

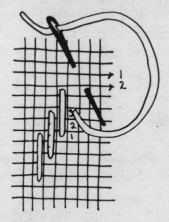

to work when you are going up toward the top of your canvas.

Moving Down

Moving down in a flame stitch, your needle travels much farther under the canvas—under six threads (seven holes) for each stitch. It seems strange until you get used to it. By continuing to stitch in this manner across the canvas, you are establishing your design.

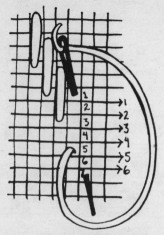

The flame stitch can be a "regular flame" or an "irregular flame."

Set up your pattern by stitching a series of flames across your canvas from end to end. Work this row in one color.

Regular flame

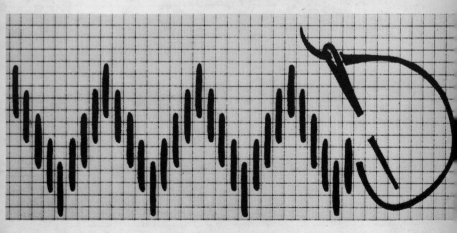

Irregular flame

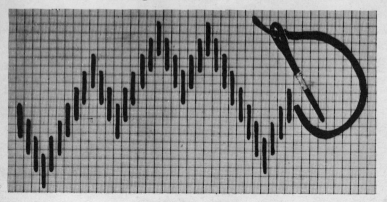

Copy the row you have established, using another color. Start the second line by bringing your needle up from the back to the front of your canvas in the *same hole* as the top of the stitch in the first row.

Start here →

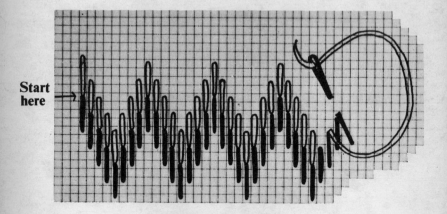

Bring your needle up at **A** and down through **B,** which is the fifth hole, as in the first row. Bring it up through **C,**

down through **D,** and up through **E.** In this way you are
copying your first row of stitching. Continue to the end of
the canvas in your second color.

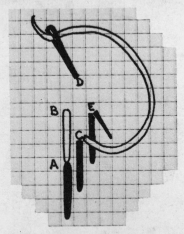

Repeat each row from one side of the canvas to the
other in this manner, building your pattern until the
peaks are hitting the line you drew (it doesn't matter if
your stitch is a few rows over or under the line).

Now, turn your canvas upside down, so the finished
part is close to you. Work the other half of your canvas in
the same manner, copying the established rows.

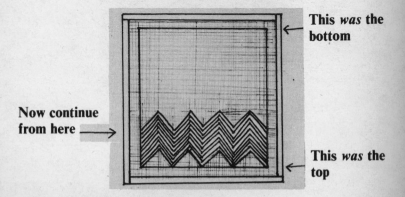

Now the only stitching left is filling in the edges at the top and bottom of your canvas. This is done by stitching in the next color as if doing a complete row across. But when you reach the finish line (the highest peak), you make the stitch only long enough to reach the peak, usually over two threads of canvas.

Each pattern in this book diagrams exactly how to stitch to fill in.

2nd fill-in row ———→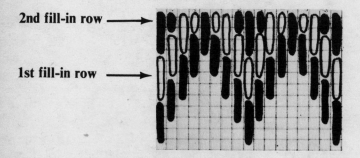

1st fill-in row ———→

Correcting Mistakes

Mistakes are common but easy to correct. If you discover a mistake in a row you are still working on:

1. Unthread your needle.

2. Using the eye end of your needle, pull your stitches out one by one until you reach the mistake.

3. Rethread your needle and start stitching again.

The most common mistake is a skipped hole at the peak of a design—watch out!

There are two ways a hole is skipped—one will throw the entire pattern off, the other will only leave a thread showing.

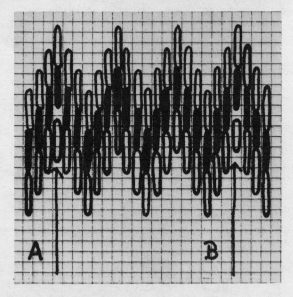

Skipping a hole and still counting five holes will throw every row off. (See A)

Skipping a hole but placing the bottom of the stitch in the right hole will only leave a space, which is easy to fill in. (See B)

If you find a mistake somewhere in the middle of your canvas and have repeated it in many rows, you have two choices:

1. Cut out the incorrect stitch (or stitches) all the way down to the mistake. Pull out several stitches on each side of this stitch so that yarn ends can be secured, and fill in stitches in appropriate colors.

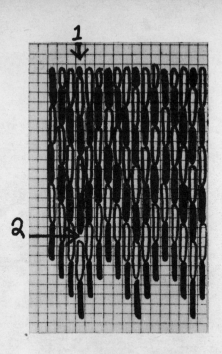

2. Put in a longer stitch right over existing stitch to fill in skipped thread.

The choice depends on your personality. If you can't stand the imperfection, follow the first method. If you feel, as I do, that handwork need not be perfect, the second choice is the simplest.

1

2

3

4

A   B   C

Patchwork Sampler

Now you are ready to start your first Bargello. A *patchwork* of a variety of patterns is fun and rewarding to do. Creating a sampler will give you a chance to try most of the stitches in this book in small areas. You will have a surprisingly beautiful piece of needlework when you have reached the end of the book.

A portion of the sampler shown here is reproduced on

D   E

the cover of the book to show color suggestions. You can follow that or use your own color preference.

To prepare your canvas:

1. Cut No. 12 canvas 19¾″ × 12½″ and tape.

2. Mark off (with your indelible pen) five 2¾″ sections across the top of your canvas and four 2¾″ sections down the side of your canvas.

3. Draw straight lines (along the threads of the canvas) so that you have twenty 2¾″ squares, a total size of 13¾″ × 11″ rectangle.

4. Choose your yarn: three colors—three shades of each color, or two colors (three shades of each) plus black and/or white.

5. Center each pattern in its square. Work each pattern as if it were going to stand alone.

6. Key

1A. Diagonal curve broken by flames (p. 37)

1B. Hearts (p. 52)

1C. Curving design (p. 28)

1D. Diamond geometric (p. 49)

1E. Large curve (p. 30)

2A. Middle size of diamonds worked horizontally (p. 55)

2B. Dramatic geometric (p. 48)

2C. Gobelin (p. 26)

2D. Long diagonal curve (p. 36)

2E. Gobelin border (p. 57)

3A. Big tulip (p. 53)

3B. Diamond shadow box (p. 46)

3C. Regular flame (p. 13)

3D. Small tulip (p. 54)

3E. Small scallop (p. 29)

4A. Arrows (p. 55)

4B. Curved geometric (p. 50)

4C. Diagonal stripe (p. 41)

4D. Two-way curve (p. 34)

4E. Florentine variation (p. 47)

Bargello Patterns

The easiest Bargello patterns are variations of the flame stitch. These patterns are all set up by working one row across your canvas to establish the pattern, then "copying" this row. Some of the patterns use groups of stitches instead of a single stitch.

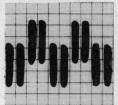

Other patterns don't move up and down over the standard two threads of the canvas. They move one thread up or down.

Brick Stitch

The *brick stitch* is as basic as the flame stitch and almost the same. Instead of going up many stitches then down many stitches, you go up three holes then down three holes repeatedly across your canvas.

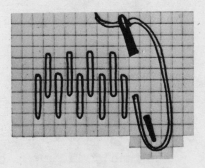

Worked in two or more colors this makes a simple but attractive pattern. Worked in one color it makes a great background stitch.

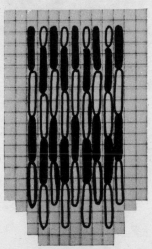

This variation of the brick stitch looks bolder. Worked in two or more colors, it's a neat pattern. Worked in one color it makes a good background stitch.

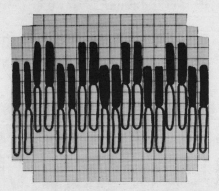

Flame Variations

This pattern is a flame-type design, with stitches worked in groups of two. Like the basic flame, it can be even or uneven, with peaks as high as you want them to go. Use two or more colors.

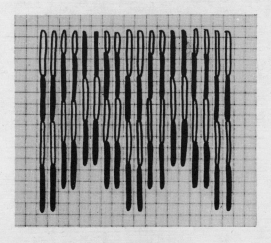

26

This pattern moves up and down only one hole in places, three holes in other places. It can be stretched so one long peak covers the whole width of the canvas or it can be repeated several times. Use two or more colors.

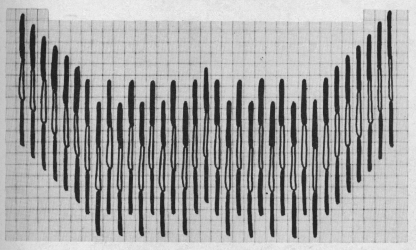

Gobelin Stitch

The *gobelin stitch* is achieved by working over four threads of canvas in straight rows. The effect can be changed by coloring.

Lines of color make an attractive pattern, using the gobelin stitch. You can use as few as two colors or as many as you can think of.

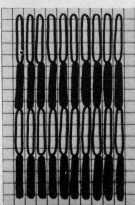

27

Check is achieved by using two shades of a color or two different colors.

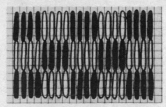

Gingham check is achieved by using a dark shade, medium shade, and white.

**1st Row
Dark-medium-
dark-medium
2nd Row
Medium-white-
medium-white
3rd Row
Repeat 1st row**
**4th Row
Repeat 2nd row**

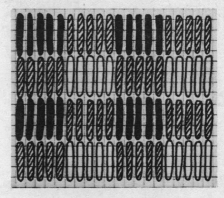

Curves

Curves are achieved by grouping stitches like this:

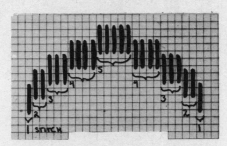

After each stitch or group of stitches you move up or down three holes as you did in the flame stitch.

A lovely curving design looks very soft. Work in four or five shades of one color, starting with a light shade and getting darker.

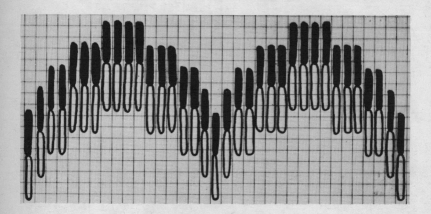

This pattern moves up and down one hole at a time and has groups of stitches. It has a nice curve.

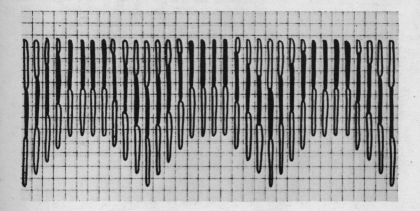

Use two or more colors. A few shades of three colors like pinks, blues, and lavenders will look very soft.

Here's a more condensed version.

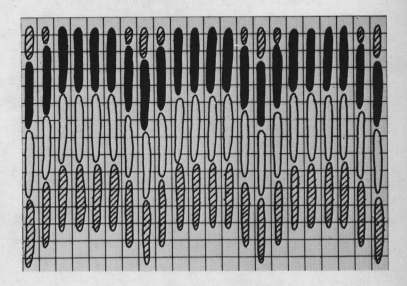

This small scallop is a very pretty pattern. Work in lots of shades of one color plus one sharply contrasting color or two contrasting colors.

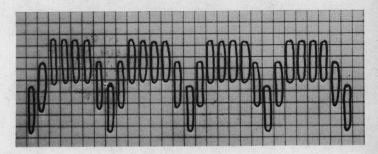

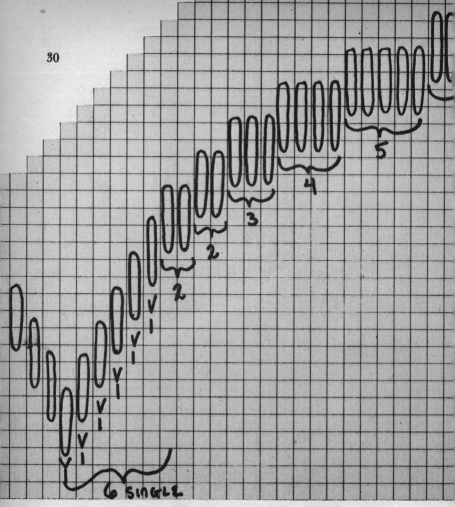

A large curve is very dramatic. It can be enlarged to stretch across the entire width of your canvas by increasing the number of stitches and stitch groups.

1. Figure the length you want your finished canvas.

2. Multiply the number of inches by the holes per inch—twelve inches by twelve holes = 144 holes.

3. Figure how many stitch groups you need to fill 144 holes.

Use four or five shades of two colors plus an accent to separate the color groups.

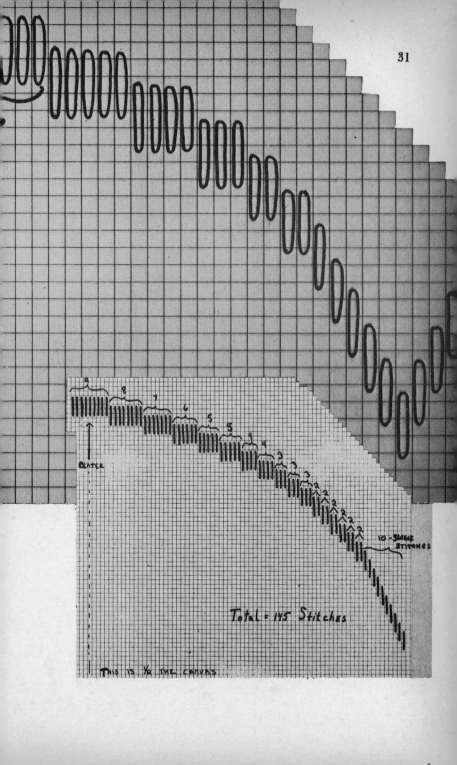

CENTER

9
8
7
6
5
5
4
3
3
2
2
2
2
2

10 - SINGLE
STITCHES

Total = 145 Stitches

THIS IS ½ THE CANVAS

Curve and Flame Combinations

This pattern combines a curve and a flame stitch. Three shades of three colors work well, but any number of colors can be used.

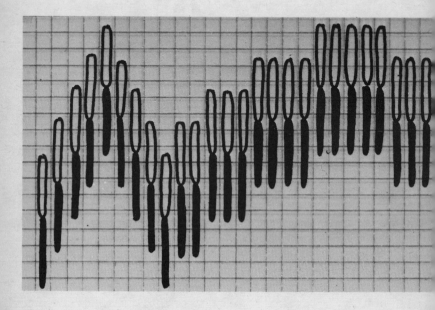

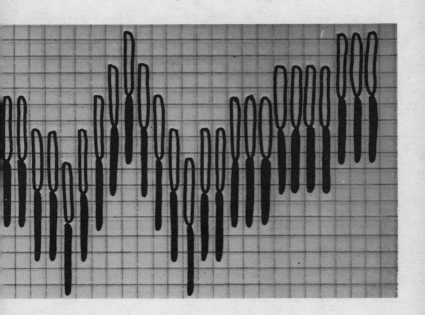

This two-way curve has no up or down side. Try using three shades of one color this way: light, medium, dark, medium, light, medium, dark. This will keep the pattern from having a top or a bottom.

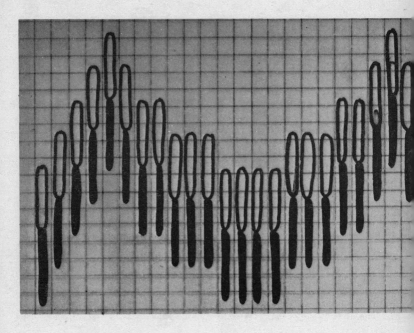

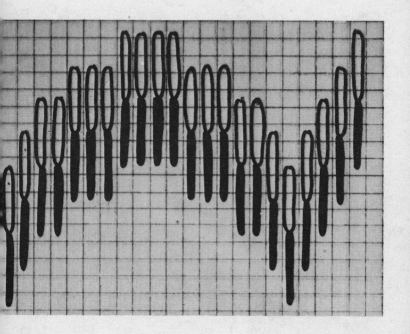

Another attractive pattern is a long diagonal curve from lower left corner of canvas to upper right corner. Use two or more colors.

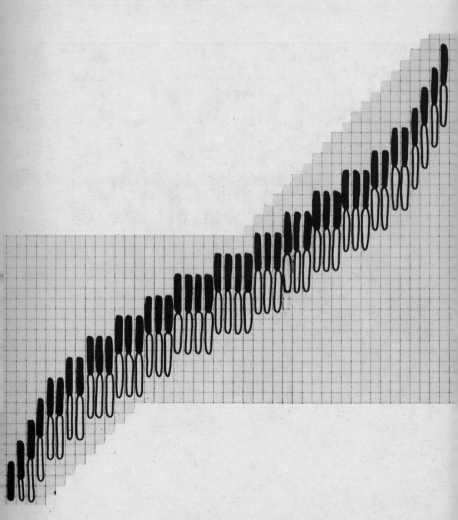

Here's another diagonal curve broken by flames. Use two or more colors.

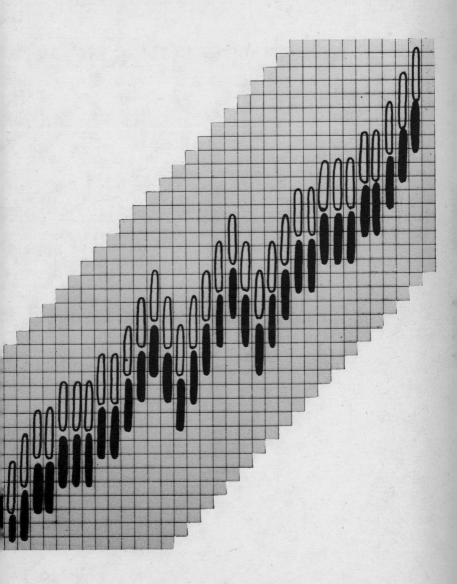

Start at the bottom center of your canvas for this pattern and work from center to right side, then from center to left side. Use two or more colors.

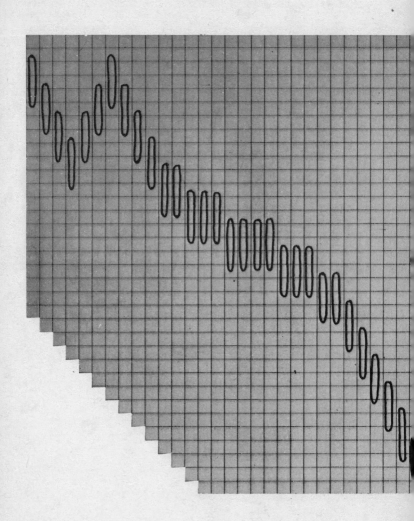

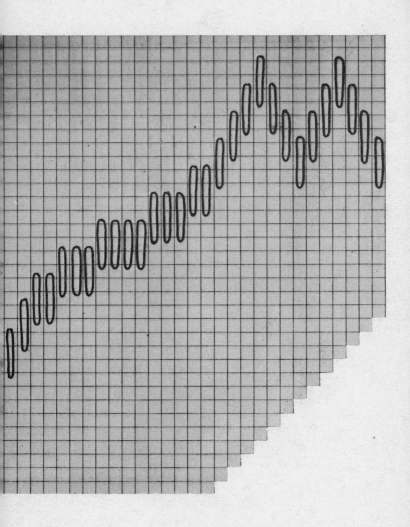

Patterns Using Varying Stitch Lengths

Stitch size may vary in many Bargello patterns. Instead of going over the standard four threads, you may go over two threads or over six or eight.

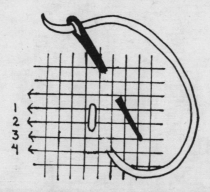

The following patterns are worked by establishing a line across the canvas, using a variety of stitch lengths.

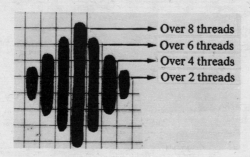

Over 8 threads
Over 6 threads
Over 4 threads
Over 2 threads

3

The diagonal stripe, using varying stitch lengths, is great in many bold colors: Red, bright yellow, blue, bright green, repeat.

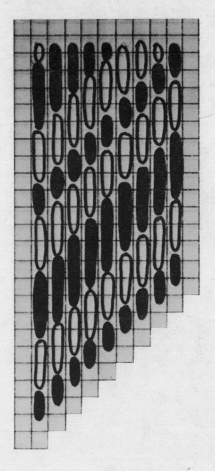

Here is another diagonal stripe in varying stitch lengths. In this pattern the stitches are in groups of two. Work in two or more colors.

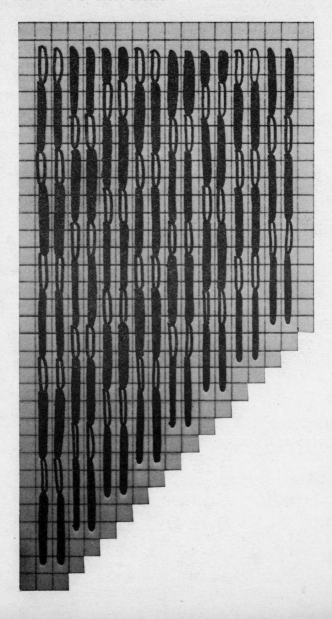

This is similar to the brick stitch, but uses varying stitch lengths. Work in two or more colors.

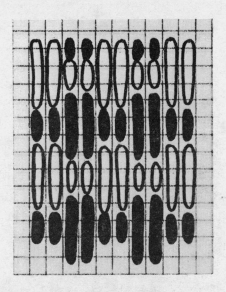

This is like the gobelin stitch, but uses varying stitch lengths. Work in two or more colors.

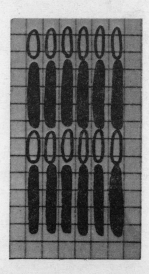

Here is a flame-type pattern, which is smooth because it moves up and down only one hole. Work in two contrasting colors for a bold look. Use many shades of one color for the long stitches and a contrasting color for the short.

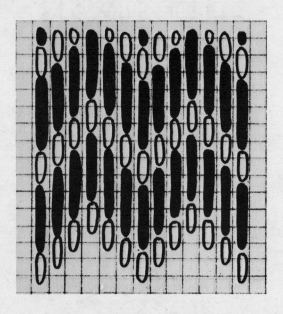

Geometric Patterns

Geometric patterns are more difficult because you can't just copy an established line. There is more figuring and counting than in the previous patterns, but the result can be worth the work.

Count each pattern carefully. Make sure the center of your design is in the dead center of your canvas.

Diamond Shadow Box

Work diamonds across canvas, making sure to skip one hole between each diamond. Fill in outline—shadow.

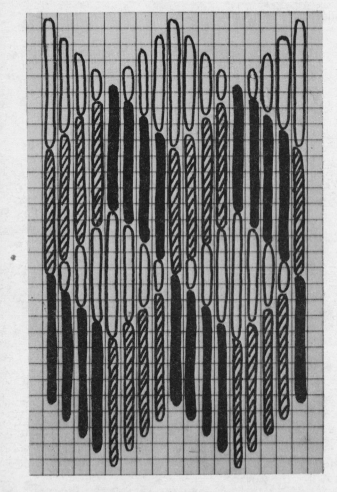

The next row of diamonds will fall into place.

Work in three colors, using two shades of one color (a dark and a medium) and one contrasting color.

Florentine Variation

This pattern has a very traditional look. It is similar to Bargello designs found on Florentine antique furniture in museums. However, this version is quite easy. Each stitch is worked over either six or two threads of canvas.

For the first row copy the graph carefully. In the next row (and all following rows) make a short stitch where there is a long one above, and a long stitch where there is a short one above.

Work in several shades of one color. Work every second row in a sharp contrasting color.

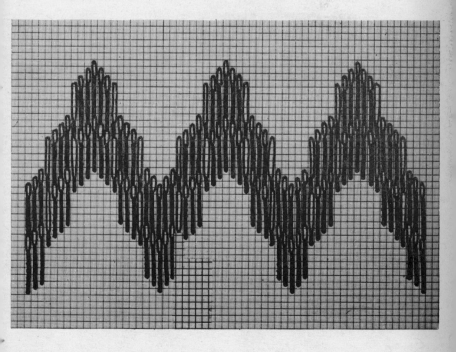

Geometrics

To work this dramatic geometric, establish an outline across your canvas, then fill in center. Work in two or three colors.

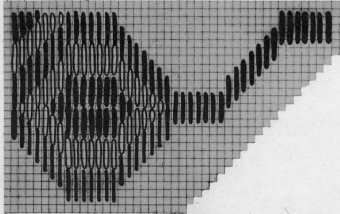

Work this variation by establishing the outline across the canvas. Work in as many as eight colors.

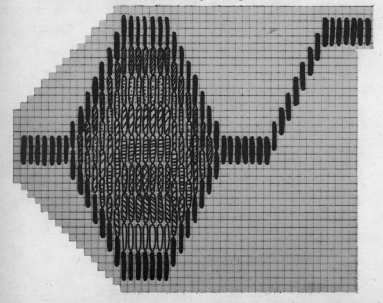

Diamond Geometric

A diamond geometric is really exciting. It can be worked by establishing a line across the canvas. Watch out for that long stitch! Work in four colors.

This is a very neat diamond geometric on a smaller scale with each stitch worked over only two threads of canvas. Work in two colors or up to four colors.

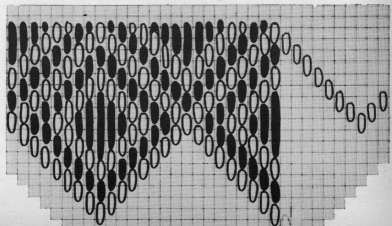

Curved Geometric

Here is a curved geometric that looks almost flower-like. It's very easy to do. Establish one line from the center of your canvas up and one line from the center down. Work in three colors for a flower look.

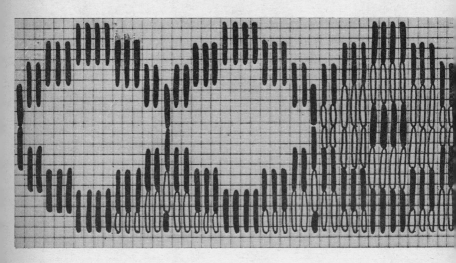

Allover Patterns

Hearts, flowers, or allover patterns are a surprise in Bargello. They are much more delicate than most Bargello designs.

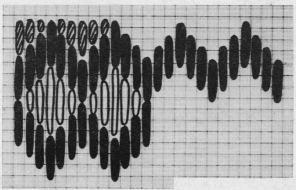

Hearts

Hearts are easy, but you must keep count. Establish a line across your canvas. Work in two colors.

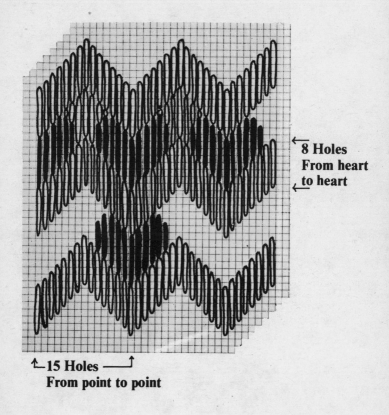

← 8 Holes
From heart
← to heart

↑—15 Holes ——↑
From point to point

Flowers

The tulip is a beautiful pattern but it has no connecting line. Each stitch is a single brick type. You must count the number of stitches between each flower horizontally and diagonally.

Work tulip in two flower shades (two pinks, two yellows, two reds, two lavenders). Work leaves in two greens. Work background in any single shade—black, white, or color.

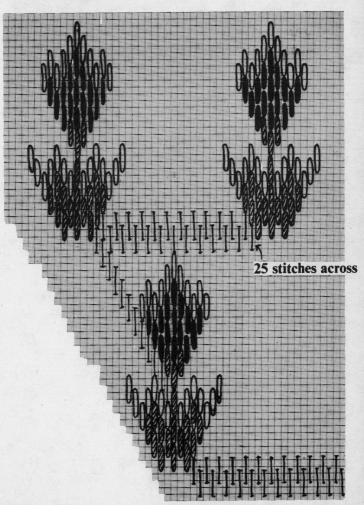

25 stitches across

Here is a smaller tulip pattern. Each stitch is over three threads of canvas and moves up one hole. But watch out for the center of the tulip where the stitches are grouped two together.

As with larger tulip, work tulip in two flower shades (two pinks, two yellows, two reds, two lavenders). Work leaves in one green. Work background in any single shade—black, white, or color.

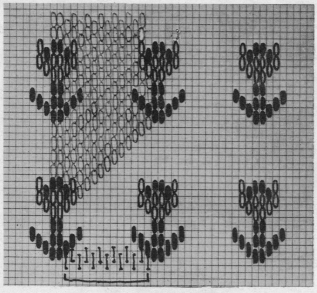

13 STITCHES ACROSS
BETWEEN TULIPS

Diamonds

Use Bargello to make diamonds in varying sizes. Work them in two colors for a neat geometric pattern. Three colors give a harlequin effect. Work in one color for a background stitch.

To outline a diamond completely, establish one outline

row, then fill in a row of diamonds. The next outline will fall into place. Work in two colors.

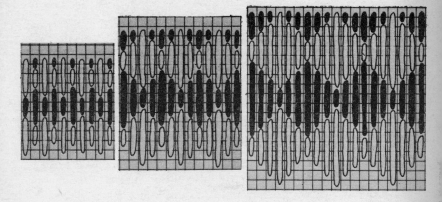

Arrows

Arrows in contrasting colors are very dramatic. You can establish a row across your canvas and follow it in varying stitch lengths. Work in two colors. Or use many colors for a very graphic effect.

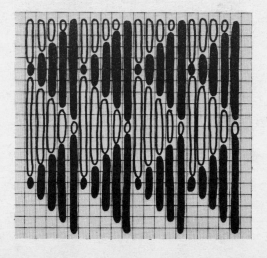

Borders

A border can surround any Bargello or needlepoint design to make it more unique and more finished.

Leave enough canvas around your design to add a border. Work your center pattern first, then, using one or more colors in your pattern, work the border. The corners are the only tricky part; they are joined diagonally. You have to decrease the length of each stitch by one hole when you work the corners.

This is a simple gobelin border. Using two shades of a color it forms a shadow box.

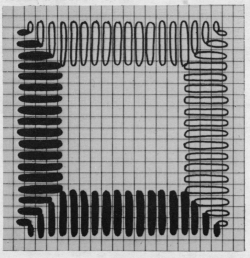

A gobelin stitch in varying sizes makes a very bold triple border. Work in two or three colors.

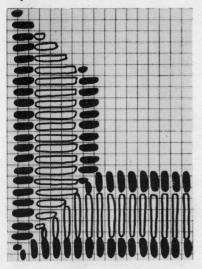

The scallop pattern border is attractive when worked in two colors.

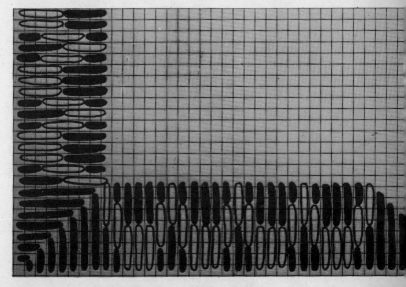

Box borders

These patterns must be square. Draw center lines on the canvas and one outside line. Draw diagonal lines from corner to corner, across center point. Work each section in a pie-shape wedge decreasing toward the center. (See graphs.) There will be eight wedges.

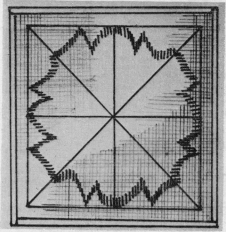

Start by working from the bottom line in the center to the right side until you reach the diagonal line. Next copy from the center to the left side. Turning your canvas as if each side were the bottom, copy this row on each of the three other sides. In this way, you form a box of Bargello.

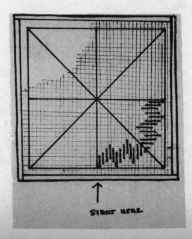

START HERE

Work these patterns with a strong color as the first row and several shades toward the center. Use only *one* contrasting color from the first row to the outer edges to strengthen the pattern feeling.

This pattern was designed by Mimi Hoenig.

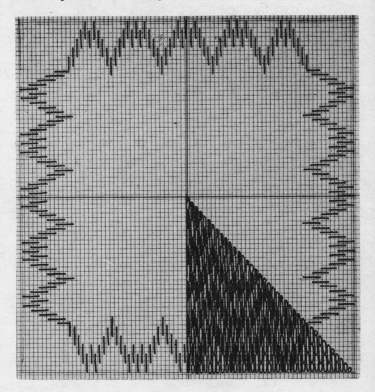

Here is a variation on the box technique using a curved line for the basic pattern.

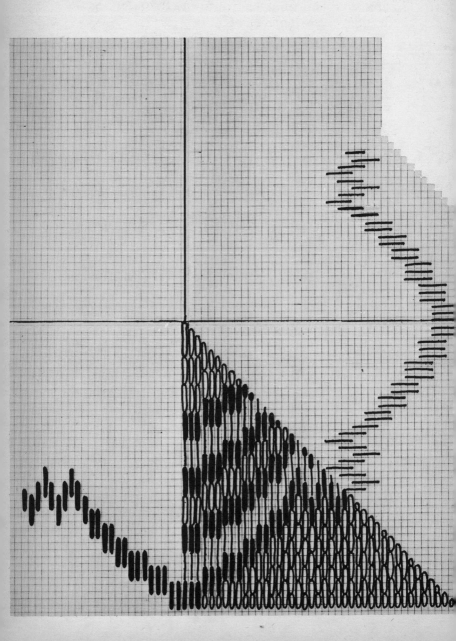

Un-Bargello

I call it *un-Bargello* when Bargello stitches are used on a painted canvas, normally intended for needlepoint. You're doing un-Bargello when you use a Bargello stitch for the background of a needlepoint (I have indicated which patterns work well as backgrounds). Un-Bargello is also when you turn your canvas sideways so some stitches are horizontal.

The following pages show an un-Bargello flower garden indicating stitches that can be used, with a graph of each stitch indicated and a detail of how to work a flower. You can apply this technique to almost any painted canvas.

Colors

- Use five colors for flowers.
- Work each flower in one solid color.
- Use one green for stems and leaves.
- Use one color for background.

Flowers	Leaves	Background
1 Red Orange Fuchsia Bright yellow Marigold	Grass green	White
2 Cornflower blue Lavender Bright yellow Turquoise Lilac	Olive green	White or light blue
3 Clear pink Cornflower blue Yellow Lavender Marigold	Bright green	White or black

1. Stems

Use a satin stitch. Stitch horizontally, working from left to right, filling in stem outline, covering as many holes as necessary to do so.

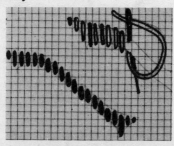

2. Leaves

Satin stitch. Work from center of leaf to outer edge. Work vertically or horizontally.

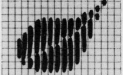

3. Flowers

Use brick stitch, working over four threads of canvas.

4. Flowers

Use very small brick stitch over two threads of canvas.

5. Flowers

Use brick-type stitch in groups of two over four threads.

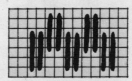

6. Flower

Establish the first curve in the center of flower. Copy this curved row, ending stitches wherever they hit the outside line of flower regardless of the length the stitch will be.

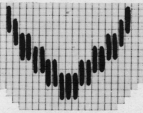

7. Flower centers

Dots indicate needlepoint stitch.

Stripes indicate satin stitch (as used on stems and leaves).

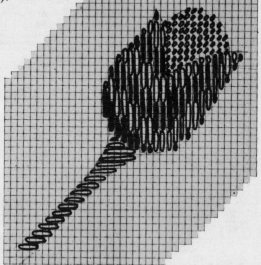

8. Background

Use brick stitch over four threads of canvas. Work horizontally.

Needlepoint surrounded by Bargello is a very beautiful pattern and not difficult. Establish a line of Bargello across your canvas from the center toward the top, and a line from the center down. The rest of the Bargello falls into place. The centers are needlepoint.

Work Bargello in four shades of green (or any color you love). Work needlepoint roses in three shades of pink (or yellow or blue or red). Use white for background of rose and the darkest green for stems and leaves.

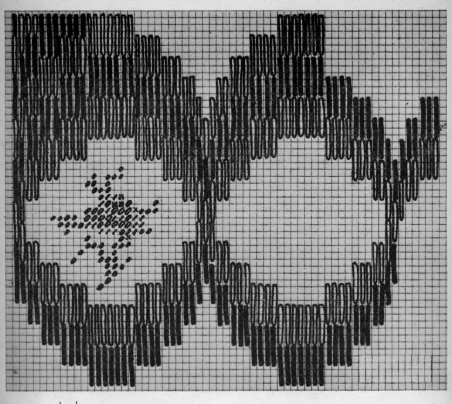

●	Green
O	Lightest flower color
/	Medium flower color
×	Darkest flower color
	Needlepoint background color

Regular Needlepoint

The *continental stitch* is the easiest needlepoint stitch for center of flowers.

For the best result, separate yarn and use two ply on No. 12 or No. 14 canvas.

- *Needlepoint* is always a diagonal stitch.
- Every stitch must go in the same direction.
- Each stitch covers only one cross of canvas.
- Start at the right side of your canvas.
- Bring needle up from back to front of your canvas.
- Hold and work over the end of yarn as you do in Bargello.

- When one row is completed turn your canvas upside down and work back in the same manner, filling every hole and covering every cross of canvas.

Shaped Pillows

Sketch an outline on paper. Fold it in half and cut it out so both sides are the same. Place the center fold in between the canvas threads in center of canvas. First outline one side, then the other with indelible marker.

Let the shape you have chosen determine the Bargello pattern. Use one of the patterns in the book or make up your own. Do some parts in needlepoint if details (eyes, mouth, and so forth) are needed. Start your Bargello on the *center* row; work from the center to the right, then copy on the left side.

This fish is worked in a smaller version of the two-way curve pattern on page 34. The first row is worked one third of the distance from the front of the fish, leaving the first third for a needlepoint face.

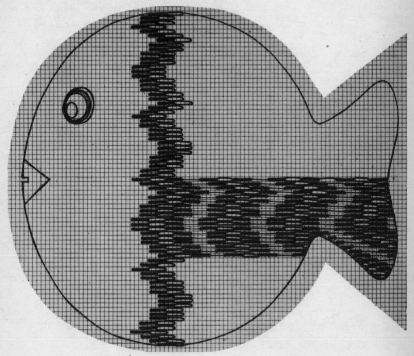

Work in three shades of many bright colors for a rainbow fish.

Stitch loops on top for fins. (See chapter on Blocking and Finishing.)

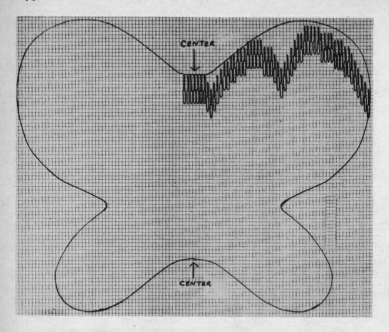

The butterfly is a free-flowing design determined by the shape of the outline.

Work in three shades of blue, green, and yellow or three shades of pink, orange, and yellow.

Put antennas on the butterfly.

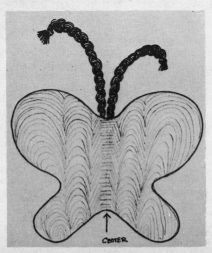

Any pattern can be used for a Christmas stocking—the bolder the better.

Work in red and white or red, white, and green. Work two rows of each color for a bold look.

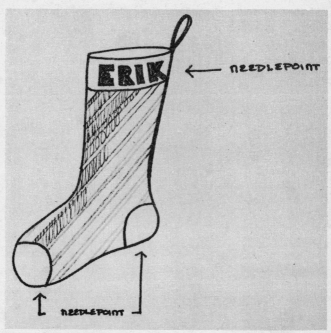

See page 41 for stripe pattern shown.

Needlepoint the heel and toe. Use one color for the top two inches for a cuff. Use a Bargello pattern for the rest of the stocking.

Blocking and Finishing

Blocking

You have just finished stitching your Bargello. Now you'll need to block it.

Materials
- A piece of plywood larger than your canvas.
- A towel or piece of cotton fabric to cover board.
- Rustproof pushpins or T pins.
- A damp cotton press cloth.
- An iron.

1. Cover the board with a towel or fabric, stapling it to the back of the board.
2. Place your canvas on the board, cover with the damp cloth and press. (It's easier to shape your canvas while it's damp.)

3. Pin canvas to board, pulling to square it off and return to its original shape.

4. Place pins in canvas or tape—*never* in embroidered part of canvas.

5. Pin in the following sequence:

  a. upper left (1a) and lower right (1b) corners; **b.** upper right (1c) and lower left (1d) corners; **c.** centers 2a and 2b, 2c and 2d; **d.** all around at two-inch intervals.

6. Cover with a very damp cloth and press by putting iron up and down. Don't slide it.

7. Leave your Bargello pinned on the board for about twelve hours or until it's completely dry.

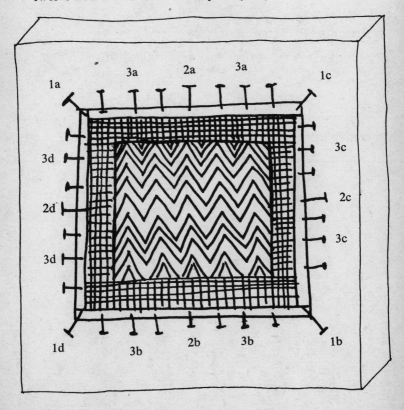

Finishing a Pillow

Materials
- Fabric for backing—about one half a yard for an average pillow.
- Polyester fiberfill or premade inner pillow for stuffing.
- Extra yarn for tassels or overcasting.

1. Block.

2. Place right side of Bargello to right side of fabric.

3. Pin all around on three sides.

4. Machine stitch on edge of Bargello on three sides, catching the tiniest bit of embroidery.

5. Trim edges three quarters of an inch from stitching on the three sides, one inch on the unsewn side.

6. Turn right side out.

7. Fill pillow with premade pillow or stuff with fiberfill (make sure you fill the corners).

8. Turn open side in. Pin and stitch closed by hand.

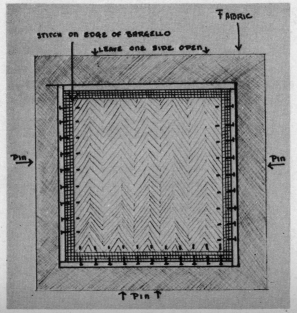

Tassels

Materials
- One ounce plus two strands of yarn (more for larger tassels) in colors to match your pillow.

- Scissors and needle.

1. Take six full-length (sixty-inch) strands of yarn and fold in half three times.

2. Using a half piece of yarn, knot in center of the folded yarn.

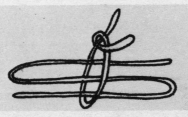

3. Thread needle with remaining half piece of yarn and twist around tassel. Sew through twist to secure end.

4. Cut ends even.

Finishing a Ruffled Pillow

Materials
• One and one-half yards of fabric for backing and ruffle.
• Polyester fiberfill or premade inner pillow for stuffing.

1. Block.

2. Cut three widths of eight-inch wide fabric (wider if you want a wider ruffle).

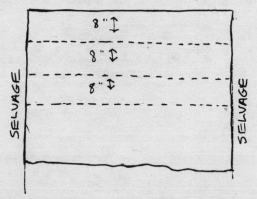

3. Sew strips together to form a large circle.

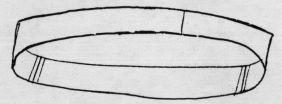

4. Fold in half (four inches wide) with right side out.

5. Gather up along cut edge to fit around outside of your Bargello.

6. With folded edge facing the center of your Bargello (on the right side), pin along gathering line of ruffle and the edge of Bargello.

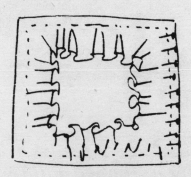

7. Machine stitch on gathering line, catching a tiny bit of Bargello.

8. Unpin. Then pin pillow backing over ruffle (right side facing right side of Bargello with ruffle sandwiched in between).

9. Machine stitch over same line on three sides.

10. Follow remaining directions for finishing pillow.

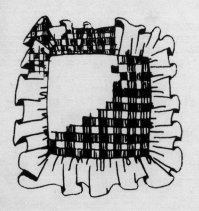

Gingham check gobelin pillow with matching ruffle and backing.

See page 27 for gingham check stitch.

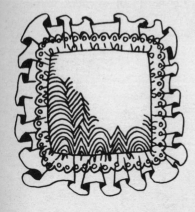

Gather eyelet with the fabric ruffle to make a very pretty bedroom pillow—or use ribbon with fabric or alone.

Finishing a Shaped Pillow, Animal, or Doll

Materials
- Fabric for backing—about one-half yard (felt works well).
- Polyester fiberfill for stuffing.
- One ounce or more of yarn to match your Bargello.

1. Block.
2. Machine stitch around edges of finished Bargello.
3. Cut canvas three quarters of an inch from finished edge all around.
4. Cut backing the same size and shape.
5. Start at center top by turning canvas back to finished edge. Pin to backing. Pin a few inches.
6. Overcast, using yarn and tapestry needle, keeping your stitches very close together.
7. Pin a few inches more, then overcast, going from the top center down one side then from top center to the other side, leaving bottom open.

8. Stuff with fiberfill, making sure all corners are filled.

9. Close bottom by overcasting.

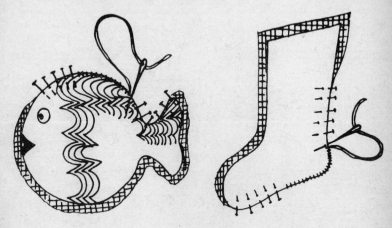

Finishing a Bag or Eyeglass Case

Materials
- One eighth of a yard of fabric—silk or thin cotton.
- Yarn to match your Bargello.
- Needle and thread.

1. Block.

2. Machine stitch around edges of finished Bargello.

3. Cut three quarters of an inch from finished edge all around.

4. Turn right sides out.

5. Fold canvas in until only finished Bargello shows. Pin.

6. Overcast edges with yarn.

7. Machine stitch lining the same size.

8. Tuck lining inside bag (or eyeglass case).

9. Hand stitch along the edges with needle and cotton thread.

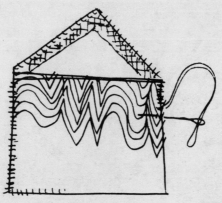

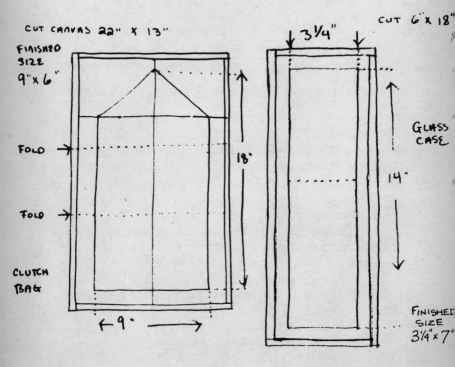

CUT CANVAS 22" x 13"

CUT 6" x 18"

FINISHED
SIZE
9" x 6"

3 1/4"

FOLD

FOLD

CLUTCH
BAG

← 9" →

18"

GLASS
CASE

14"

FINISHED
SIZE
3 1/4" x 7"

Bargello Belt

Belts are great in Bargello. I think it's best to decide on the finished style of your belt before starting. The length and width are determined by the closure you choose. It's often easier to find a great buckle and make a belt to fit it than to try to find the right buckle for a finished belt.

The best buckles for Bargello belts are those that have two sides and clasp in the center. They eliminate the bulk of overlapping, as in a slide-through buckle, or the need of eyelets for a prong buckle.

One of the most basic buckles looks like this:

Try a great big hook and eye

You can also use a prong buckle—men seem to prefer it because it is adjustable.

The problem with this kind of buckle is that you need eyelets. Some notions stores will put eyelets in. This is the best way. Or you can use a hand punch (available in notions stores). However, I find Bargello belts too heavy for the hand punch to work well. Or you can simply remove the prong and use it as a slip-through buckle. Allow about four inches more needlework for overlap on this type of buckle.

You can also close your Bargello belt with ties and tassels.

In this case the needlework needs to be long enough to just meet in the center.

Now that you have decided on the style, cut your canvas. For a 1¾" wide belt (great for pants), cut 4" wide by about 36" long (longer for men). For a 1" wide "skinny" belt, cut 2½" wide by about 36" long. Bargello tends to "shrink up" so make your belt at least 3" longer than you need it.

Pick a pattern from the following or do your own and needle it up.

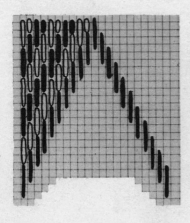
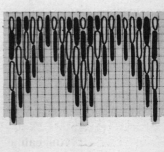
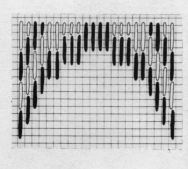
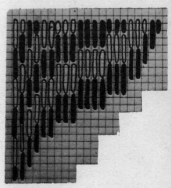

84

Other patterns that are suitable for belts:
Double Brick p. 25
Small Scallop p. 29
Diamonds p. 54
Arrows p. 55
Diagonal Stripe p. 41

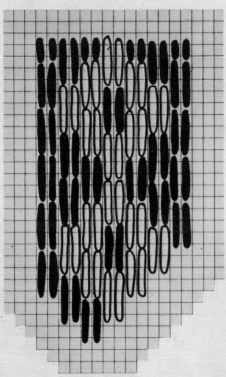

Finishing a Belt

Materials
- Grosgrain ribbon the same width as your finished stitching and about two inches longer.
- Buckle. Make sure the width corresponds to the width of your stitching.
- Needle and thread.

1. Block.
2. Cut canvas three quarters of an inch from the finished Bargello along the length.
3. Turn canvas back to finished Bargello edge. Press with a damp cloth.
4. Pin grosgrain on back over unworked canvas.
5. With cotton thread, stitch ribbon to Bargello along both lengths, using an overcasting type stitch, catching the first row of Bargello.
6. Cut ends one-half inch from stitching. Push in between ribbon and canvas and stitch closed.
7. Using your tapestry needle and yarn to match your belt, overcast the bar of your buckle to the end of the belt.

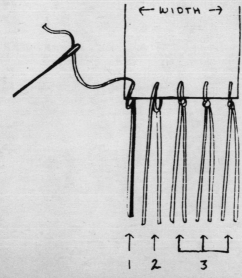

8. Or, if you are using tassels for a closure, thread your needle with a matching color yarn sixty inches long.

a. Sew yarn through width end of belt twice to form a loop.

b. Even up the yarn ends.

c. Knot yarn close to the belt.

LEAVE AS FRINGE   ONE FAT BRAID   SEVERAL BRAIDS

About the Author

Peri Wolfman is a truly "designing" woman. After graduating from Parsons School of Design in New York, she began her career by designing children's clothing, her name appearing on the Suzy Brooks label. While still designing for the garment industry, Peri took on needlepoint as her "commuter's hobby." When *Seventeen* magazine eventually discovered her needlepoint designs and featured them to be ordered by mail, department stores around the country started ordering kits for their needlework departments, and her mail-order business grew.

In late 1971, Peri Wolfman opened a needlework shop in Larchmont, New York. She soon became aware of the many problems that her patrons, many relatively new to the crafts, had when they tried to work the colorful, but complicated and rigid, patterns shown in the large, expensive, "supposedly how-to" craft books they had bought. A long-time believer in the do-your-own-thing style of needlecraft, Ms. Wolfman recognized the need for basic, inexpensive teaching books, especially for Bargello, the newly popular canvas work that fascinated and confounded so many of her patrons ... thus, BARGELLO IS EASY.

Peri Wolfman recently turned the running of her successful Larchmont store over to a new partner and is now a resident of San Francisco, where she intends to set up a studio where she can create needlepoint designs for various department stores, her mail-order catalog, and her own needlework shop back home.